ts

DK READE... is a compelling new program for beginning readers, designed in conjunction with leading literacy experts, including Dr. Linda Gambrell, Director of the School of Education at Clemson University. Dr. Gambrell has server on the board of Directors of the International Reading Association and as President of the National Reading Conference.

Beautiful illustrations and superb full-color photographs combine with engaging, easy-to-read stories to offer a fresh approach to each subject in the series. Each DK READERS is guaranteed to capture a child's interest while developing his or her reading skills, general knowledge, and love of reading.

The four levels of DK READERS are aimed at different reading abilities, enabling you to choose the books that are exactly right for your child:

**Level 1** – Beginning to read
**Level 2** – Beginning to read alone
**Level 3** – Reading alone
**Level 4** – Proficient readers

The "normal" age at which a child begins to read can be anywhere from three to eight years old, so these levels are intended only as a general guideline.

No matter which level you select, you can be sure that you are helping your child learn to read, then read to learn!

LONDON, NEW YORK, DELHI,
MUNICH, and MELBOURNE

Produced by Southern Lights
Custom Publishing

For Dorling Kindersley
**Publisher** Andrew Berkhut
**Executive Editor** Andrea Curley
**Art Director** Tina Vaughan
**Photographer** Keith Harrelson

### Reading Consultant
Linda Gambrell, Ph.D.

First American Edition, 2001
03 04 05 10 9 8 7 6 5 4 3 2
Published in the United States by Dorling Kindersley Publishing, Inc.
375 Hudson Street, New York, New York 10014

Copyright © 2001 Dorling Kindersley Limited, London

All rights reserved under International and Pan-American
Copyright Conventions. No part of this publication
may be reproduced, stored in a retrieval system,
or transmitted in any form or by any means, electronic,
mechanical, photocopying, recording, or otherwise, without
the prior written permission of the copyright owner.

Published in Great Britain by Dorling Kindersley Limited.

**Library of Congress Cataloging-in-Publication Data**

Hayward, Linda.
  A day in the life of a teacher / by Linda Hayward.-
1st American ed.
    p. cm. -- (Dorling Kindersley readers)
  Audience: "Level, preschool-grade 1."
  ISBN 0-7894-7368-2   ISBN 0-7894-7367-4 (pbk.)
  1. Elementary school teachers--Juvenile literature. 2. Elementary
school teaching--Juvenile literature. [1.Teachers 2. Schools
3. Occupations.] I. Title. II. Series.

LB1776 H39 2001
372.11--dc21
                                                            00-055522

Printed and bound in China by L. Rex Printing Co., Ltd.

The characters and events in this story are fictional and do not
represent real persons or events. The author would like to thank Janis
Liss for her help.
            All other images © Dorling Kindersley
      For further information see: www.dkimages.com

Discover more at

# www.dk.com

DK READERS

BEGINNING
1
TO READ

# A Day in the Life of a Teacher

Written by Linda Hayward

DK
DK Publishing, Inc.

109498

 7:00 a.m.

It is time to go to school.
The Hill family gets ready.
Eric and Jason finish breakfast.
Jan Hill fills her tote bag.

Two books,
one lunch,
28 toy fish!

tote bag

Jan teaches second grade.

Jan drives to school.

In the office she checks her mailbox. She picks up her attendance folder.

folder

Time to fix
the calendar!
Today is
Wednesday.

calendar

Before school,
Josh shows
Ms. Hill
his turtle.

Josh was
in her class
last year.

8:00 a.m.

The bell rings.

"Line up here!" says Ms. Hill.

Room Nine lines up.

As they come in, the students
put their homework
in the basket.

basket

Ms. Hill takes
attendance.
Ryan is absent.

# Hana's reading group practices listening skills.

What happened First?

Second?

Then?

The class is learning
about fish.
Ms. Hill passes out
the toy fish.
Then she writes a
word on the board.

dictionary

fins

Who can find
it in the
dictionary?

*Brnng!*
The fire alarm!
The class lines up
to go outside.

Walking in line
can be hard.

"No pushing!"
says Ms. Hill.

Is it safe to go
back in? Yes!
It was just
a fire drill.

Back in the room, Todd
studies spelling words.

Emily reads
from her journal.

journal

Ms. Hill asks the aide, Ms. Lee, to cut paper for art. "We need 28 of each!" she says. Ms. Hill is planning a bulletin board.

 12:00 p.m.

The teachers have lunch together.
They plan their school show.

"The third grade can sing the song about the forest," says Ms. Lopez.

12:30 p.m.

Lunch is over.
A hush falls in Room Nine.
Ms. Hill is reading
a new book of poems.

Now it is time for math.
Ms. Hill has a box.
She takes out one big red square,
one big yellow circle,
and one small yellow circle.

# What other shapes are inside?

square

1:45 p.m.

Jim and Katy learn about graphs.

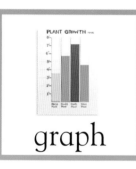

graph

Jose is working on the computer.

Rob has his octopus ready for
the bulletin board.

8 UNDERSEA STORY IDEAS

The school day is almost over.
The students pack up their
homework.

Homework
Spelling words
Science project

 3:00 p.m.

When the bell rings, everyone walks out to the buses.

Ryan's sister comes to pick up his homework. Here is a card that Ryan made for Ms. Hill.

4:30 p.m.

Jan Hill has her own
homework. Her son Eric
helps with the laundry.

Jason serves dinner. It was his turn to cook.

10:00 p.m.

Before she goes to bed,
Jan looks at
Ryan's card again.

She smiles.
She has the best job in the world!

JUV
372.11
H4275
2001

109498

# Picture Word List

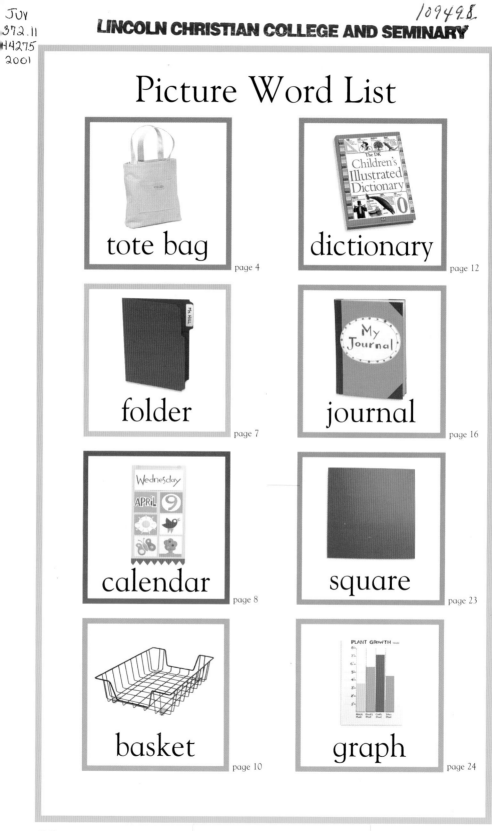

tote bag

page 4

dictionary

page 12

folder

page 7

journal

page 16

calendar

page 8

square

page 23

basket

page 10

graph

page 24

3 4711 00193 1411